Summer and the Staircase

Summer and the Staircase

Kate Foster

Illustrated by
Fran Cesarano

Collins

Contents

Chapter 1 7

Bonus: The Spriggins family 20

Chapter 2 23

Bonus: Missing posters 38

Chapter 3 41

Bonus: Real gemstones 56

Chapter 4 59

Bonus: Wonderful things for me 72

Chapter 5 75

Bonus: Animal hoarders 88

Chapter 6 91

Bonus: A retelling 104

About the author 106

About the illustrator 108

Book chat 110

Chapter 1

Summer Spriggins pedalled her shiny silver bike through the streets of her estate as fast as she could. She whizzed around corners, bounced over bumps and dips, and swerved past muttering residents. Her cheeks and nose stung in the chilly wind and her legs ached, but she was already two minutes late. Mrs Barry was not a patient person, and Summer was not very good at timekeeping.

Doing chores for Mrs Barry wasn't Summer's ideal way to spend her free time, but the little money she earned from it each week was all part of her plan.

One more hour of tidying Mrs Barry's flat meant one more envelope of money, and this meant she could finally afford the glittering opal displayed in the shop window of *Precious Rocks and Gems*.

That opal was going to put a smile not only on Summer's face, but also Dad's and her younger brother Alfie's. They were all so different. The only things they had in common were that they were each autistic, and they loved unique and precious rocks.

Their collection took up shelves and sideboards and boxes in every room of their tiny house, but Summer knew the perfect spot for the opal – on top of the fireplace. That's where Grandma's brass candlestick had sat, before it had been stolen three weeks ago.

Summer squeezed the handlebars of her bike and gritted her teeth.

Her family already had enough to deal with: Summer struggled with every subject at school, Dad worked two jobs so they could afford rent and food, and Alfie's speech therapy was not going well.

So it was terribly unfair that someone had stolen such a precious item from their home. Whoever this *someone* was had been stealing from other homes on the estate, too.

Buying the opal for her family would cheer them all up and Summer couldn't wait to make that happen.

She rounded the corner of Blockman Road where the entrance to Mrs Barry's flat was, but her stomach immediately dropped into her shoes. Sebastian Gorlay – the most unpleasant boy on the estate – was heading towards the building, and that meant one thing.

Summer applied her brakes and screeched to a halt, hopping off her bike at the same time. Sebastian smirked at her as she jogged towards him.

"You're late again," he said.

"Only by a few minutes," Summer said. "Mrs Barry could have waited for me."

He shook his head. "She's angrier than usual today as her lucky gold cat necklace has been stolen. Luckily, she called me and now I'm here to save the day."

"Well, I can take over from here," Summer said.

Sebastian threw out his arm to block Summer. "No, sorry," he said. "I need the money so I can replace my stolen watch."

"No wait, I –" Summer started, but Sebastian turned his back and walked off, nose in the air.

Summer deflated like a balloon. Words died on her tongue as she watched Sebastian disappear up the flight of stairs to Mrs Barry's flat, whistling to himself.

Now what was she going to do? She sighed. Her shoulders sagged. She plodded away, pushing her bike along beside her.

"What a disaster," she mumbled to herself. "Now I can't afford the opal and we won't be able to add it to our collection and we won't all have the happiness we deserve."

Summer kept her head down as she pushed her bike along the pavement. Her pink trainers took her step by step towards the local shops. Voices from residents rose and fell around her as she wandered along, and she caught the odd word and sentence. Conversation was mostly about their stolen possessions and the elusive thief.

"Whoever it is, they stole my antique silver serving spoon," said Mr Philpot.

"My old teddy bear is missing," grumbled Mr Johnston. "My late wife made a tartan waistcoat for it especially."

"My old cuckoo clock is gone," cried Mr McGee.

Then, another voice spoke, drawing Summer out from her slump. The voice was gentle yet eerie. It was smooth yet gravelly. It captured her attention but gave her goosebumps at the same time. Summer frowned and glanced up.

"Little girl, why do you look so sad?"

A woman peered at Summer. She had short, reddish hair and a floor-length gown that seemed to change colour in the fading winter sunshine. Her eyes were mesmerising. The brightest amber Summer had ever seen. Almost golden.

"Why do you look so sad?" the woman asked again.

Before Summer had a chance to think, words tumbled from her mouth. "I was late for my chores and now I don't have enough money to buy the opal."

How strange. Summer knew better than to speak to strangers. Why had she shared so much information?

"Oh, poor little girl," the woman said, eyes gleaming.

"Who are you?" Summer asked, intrigued. She knew most people who lived in town, but this woman was unfamiliar.

She smiled. "You may call me Amber."

"Like your eyes," Summer replied, again surprised at the sound of her voice.

"Indeed," Amber said. "This is my shop."

Amber gestured behind her, and there stood a shop. The sign above read: *Wonderful Things for Me.* Summer frowned. A whole entire shop that she'd never seen before. How odd.

Amber stood on the steps leading up to the entrance. Fairy lights glittered beyond the doorway.

Summer peeked around Amber; even though more lights twinkled inside the store, it looked somewhat gloomy inside. Summer's instincts tingled with warnings, but she couldn't put her finger on what exactly was wrong.

She was about to walk away when a smart-looking man dipped his head to Amber and entered the store, a small boy scurrying in after him.

So, instead of leaving, Summer inhaled and asked, "What do you sell?"

Amber smiled, exposing bright teeth, almost too white to be real. "Anything and everything. Wonderful things for you. Wonderful things for me."

Wonderful things? Like precious rocks?

"Why don't you come in and have a look?" Amber asked.

Summer chewed her bottom lip, then nodded. She didn't want to go home empty-handed. She wanted to replace the stolen candlestick.

"Wonderful," Amber said. "I'm sure you will find what you're looking for."

Summer leaned her bike against the wall of the shop and climbed the steps. As she passed Amber, a rush of different odours wafted over her. First flowers and mud, then the freshness of the air after rainfall, then smoke and rubbish bins. At first, Summer liked it, but soon she screwed up her nose in distaste.

With a deep breath, Summer took a step inside the shop. Pressing a hand to the money in her pocket, she allowed her eyes to adjust to the darkness ... and gasped.

Bonus: The Spriggins family

DAD

Loves rocks

Works as a mechanic

Quiet

Enjoys listening to classical music

Favourite food is pizza

SUMMER

Loves rocks

Wants to be a vet

Chatterbox

Enjoys reading scary stories

Favourite food is pasta

ALFIE

Loves rocks

Wants to be a pilot

Noisy and fidgety

Enjoys watching cartoons on TV

Favourite food is chicken nuggets

Chapter 2

It was as if everything that had ever existed in the world was crammed inside the tiny shop.

Summer admired shelves stuffed with jewellery, ornaments and toys, a table covered in crockery, cutlery and other kitchenware, and a towering cabinet filled with glassware. She gaped at framed photos and artwork on the walls and at windchimes and suncatchers hanging from the ceiling.

"Wow," she marvelled.

"Thank you," said Amber beside her.

Summer startled. Usually, she disliked being close to other people, yet it was as if Amber had cast a strange spell on her that was affecting her senses.

"Is there anything in particular you need?" Amber asked, sweeping a hand towards a table that Summer now noticed for the first time.

Upon a gold tablecloth was a display of rocks and gems. She approached, her eyes hungry as they took in all the shapes, sizes and colours.

"You're a rockhound."

Summer nodded, but was too captivated by the gems to turn away.

"I don't have any opals, but –" Amber's voice trailed off.

"But ... what?" Summer asked.

Amber narrowed her eyes at Summer, as if deciding whether to share or not. Then, in a swift motion, Amber disappeared through a doorway in the corner of the store and returned moments later, with a small parcel wrapped in golden tissue paper clasped in her hands.

Summer wiggled her hands in excitement as Amber held out the object. With a smirk, golden eyes fixed on Summer, Amber peeled back the layers of tissue paper.

"Oh my –" Summer couldn't finish the sentence.

Resting in the palm of Amber's hand was a rock slightly smaller than a golf ball. Yet, it wasn't a rock Summer recognised. The more she stared, the more it changed. One second it appeared as a diamond, the next a ruby, before catching a ray of light and morphing into a pearl. Then an amethyst. Then a quartz.

Dizzied by its everchanging form, Summer looked away. "I've never seen anything like it," she murmured.

"It's a rare Catacombite," Amber replied. "It holds magical powers that bring pure happiness to those who own it."

An incredible rock with magical powers that bring happiness? This was exactly what Summer wanted for her family. She pressed a hand to the money in her pocket, butterflies erupting in her tummy. "How much does it cost?"

Amber tilted her head to one side, studying Summer's face, her eyes sparkling extra bright. "How much do you have?"

Summer spread her money out on the table. Amber eyed it briefly, then peered over Summer's shoulder towards the entrance of the shop.

"How about," Amber began, "I give you the Catacombite for all your money and … your bicycle."

"My bike?" Summer raised her eyebrows.

"Yes. I have always wanted one." Amber licked her lips.

Summer gulped and looked at her coins, then towards the door. Could she manage without her bike? It was her only way to get to and from school, and to Mrs Barry's to help with the chores. Dad didn't have the money to buy a bus pass for Summer, so without her bike, this left walking everywhere.

Summer turned away, her eyes drawn back to the Catacombite. At first glance it appeared as a dull grey rock, but within a split-second it changed again – emerald to agate to aquamarine to zirconia to jade ….

Summer blinked, the rock's dizzying beauty sending her off-balance.

It really was magic.

Without another thought, Summer blurted, "OK."

"We have a deal?" Amber asked in a voice that was almost a hiss.

Summer swallowed and nodded. "It's a deal."

"Wonderful things for me," Amber replied. A few moments later, Amber placed the Catacombite wrapped in both gold tissue and brown paper into the palm of Summer's hand.

"Have a wonderful day, little girl," Amber said, before closing the door and shutting Summer outside.

Summer shivered. The sun had disappeared behind a blanket of angry clouds, plunging the temperature down. She should get home. Hopping down the steps, Summer went to grab her bike, but stopped.

Of course, the bike was no longer hers. She sighed, shoved the Catacombite into her pocket and retied the scarf around her neck. She had a long walk ahead of her. She patted the handlebar of her bike, which her dad had found in a skip and lovingly restored for her a few years ago. "See you around," she said to it, then headed off.

Just before she turned the corner, she looked back, wanting to see her bike one final time. Her shoes scuffed on the gravel path.

It was gone.

Amber must have taken it already. An unpleasant heaviness lingered in Summer's chest. Had she made the wrong choice?

It was too late now. She pressed a hand against the Catacombite in her pocket and sucked in a long breath of the cold air.

"It's worth it," she said to herself. "Dad and Alfie will be just as excited as I am to add this to our family collection."

Summer headed home, forcing a spring into her steps. Half an hour later, her hands and nose frozen, she reached her street. Daylight had almost disappeared, and the clouds hung even lower.

With a final flurry of energy, Summer ran the rest of the way. Flinging open the front door, she burst into the warmth of the hallway. She tore off her coat and kicked off her shoes, then opened the lounge door. Alfie and Dad were sitting on the green carpet playing a game.

"Sunner," Alfie cried, clapping. "Play."

Summer smiled and joined her family in front of the fire to play Alfie's new speech therapy game.

"You look freezing," Dad said. "And you're later than usual. How was Mrs Barry today?"

Summer avoided Dad's eyes. "Fine," she replied, deciding not to tell him about what really happened. "I bought us all a present."

With a trembling hand, she removed the Catacombite from her pocket.

"A present, for us?" Dad said. "Summer, you didn't have to do that."

Alfie squeaked, his bright brown eyes sparkling.

Summer glanced at the glaring gap on the fireplace. "It's for our collection."

Alfie clapped and jiggled on the spot.

Dad laughed, then stroked Summer's hair. "Thank you."

Summer placed the package on the carpet and peeled back the brown paper, then the gold tissue. Her hands shook, but not from the cold. She peeked up at her family.

Instead of smiles, however, Dad frowned, and Alfie screwed up his face.

"It's ... lovely," Dad said.

Lovely? It was more than lovely.

Summer stared at the Catacombite.

But all she saw was a dull grey rock.

Missing posters

STOLEN ITEM
BRASS CANDLESTICK

If found please contact:
2 8456 7870

MISSING!
GOLD CAT NECKLACE

IF FOUND PLEASE CONTACT MRS BARRY

HAVE YOU SEEN THIS TEDDY?

A SENTIMENTAL AND TREASURED ITEM. PLEASE CONTACT MR JOHNSTON WITH ANY INFORMATION.

PLEASE HELP FIND
Antique silver serving spoon

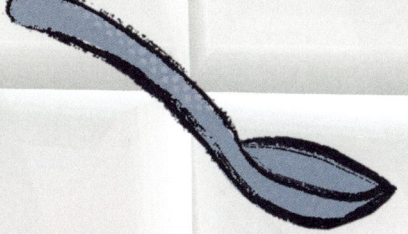

Email any information to
Mr Philpot phil.philpot@pots.com

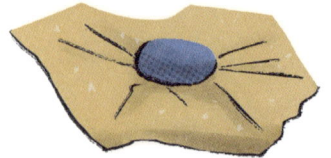

Chapter 3

"But –" Summer gritted her teeth.

"It's lovely," Dad said again. "I hope you didn't spend too much money though."

Alfie wandered away.

"But –" Summer couldn't understand it.

"Anyway, I'll start dinner while you play with Alfie," Dad said, rising to his feet.

"No, wait!" Summer exclaimed. "It's a Catacombite."

Dad smiled. "Catacombite? I've never heard of that."

"It's rare and magic. Keep looking at it and you'll see," Summer urged him.

Dad leaned over and joined Summer studying the rock. The longer they looked, the duller and greyer the rock seemed to become. It matched the colour of the clouds outside.

"What am I looking for?" Dad asked.

"It changes," Summer said, her voice quivering as tears threatened to fall.

"Changes how?" Dad asked.

"In the shop, it kept changing colour and shape."

"Right," Dad replied. "I'll go and start chopping the vegetables for supper, but call me when you notice it changing."

As Dad padded out of the room, Summer leaned back against the sofa. Maybe the changes had something to do with the light. She lifted the Catacombite, holding it up towards the lamplight. Then she tried holding it by the glow of the fire. But no. Nothing changed.

"Play," Alfie said.

"One second," Summer replied. "I need to check something."

With a ball of confusion growing in her tummy, Summer sat at Dad's computer in the corner of the room and opened a search page. She typed in *CATACOMBITE*, but no results returned. She tried a different spelling and then another, but still found nothing.

She typed in 'rock that changes appearance' but the results she saw onscreen looked nothing like the Catacombite.

Alfie's playful sounds and the *chop chop* of Dad cutting veggies in the kitchen mixed with the buzzing of the electric lamp and the hissing of the radiator. Summer was overloading.

She thought back to the shop, to Amber, and to how strange she'd felt there. Emotions swirled and grew inside her tummy, developing into anger and rage.

A tear trickled down her cheek, followed by another and another.

The rock lay on the floor, still grey, still dull.

Amber had tricked her.

Despite it being Saturday, Summer woke extra early to check on the rock's appearance. But it was still the same dull grey. Summer's mind whirled with memories of the shop and Amber.

All her hard-earned money *and* her bike gone.

Amber had tricked her.

Amber had lied to her.

If there was one thing Summer disliked more than anything, it was dishonesty. She knew what she had to do.

Summer would return the Catacombite and get her money and bike back.

After getting dressed, she grabbed the rock, not bothering to wrap it back up, and shoved it in her pocket. With coat, scarf and gloves on, she opened the front door and stepped outside. The clouds remained dark and low, and a few spots of rain fell. Summer shivered and headed off, on foot.

As she walked, she rehearsed what she would say.

"Hi, Amber –"

Was saying *hi* too friendly? Maybe.

"Hello, Amber."

Yes, that was better. More formal.

"Hello, Amber. I don't know if you remember me, but yesterday you sold me this." Summer practised holding the rock out in front of her. "It is not the same one you showed me in the shop."

Next would come the big request.

"I would like my money and my bike back."

Maybe she should say *please*. Even though she didn't feel like being polite, Dad always insisted on good manners.

"I would like my money and my bike back, please."

Summer repeated this a few times until she felt ready. Her hands made tight fists in her gloves. She did not like any type of confrontation. If she hadn't lost her bike and if the empty spot on the fireplace wasn't still there, she probably wouldn't be doing this.

As Summer rounded the corner, nausea danced in her belly. She stomped towards the shop door.

The closer she got, however, the slower she went.

The shop sign was gone. The windows were dirty. No fairy lights twinkled outside or inside, and piles of unopened envelopes were scattered on the top step.

Summer squatted and picked up one of the letters. It was addressed to 'The Occupier', as were all the others.

What was going on?

Summer stood, noticing then that the shop door was ajar. She pushed it gently, dread building in her chest. The door creaked open. She swallowed as the tiny, empty shop came into view.

"Gone," she said under her breath.

She took a tentative step forward, kicking aside more unopened letters. Her footsteps echoed in the emptiness.

"Everything. It's all gone."

No shelves, no cabinets. No jewellery, no kitchenware. Nothing displayed in the windows and nothing hanging from the ceiling.

Summer spun slowly in a circle, tears falling.

Not only had Amber tricked her, but she had also vanished, taking everything with her.

Summer crumpled into a ball on the floor and sobbed.

How could she have been so silly? Her instincts had told her something wasn't right with the shop, with Amber. Why had she ignored them?

Then there was the man and his son, the ones who'd entered before her yesterday. She tried to remember seeing them in the shop, but she couldn't. Where had they gone? She was usually so aware of people around her, but she'd been mesmerised by everything crammed into the space, especially the table of rocks and gems.

After several minutes, Summer sat up and dusted off her coat. Though she was angry with Amber, she was angrier with herself.

As that anger grew, she climbed to her feet, her breath coming faster.

It wasn't fair. None of it.

Summer pulled the rock from her pocket and held it up.

Dull. Grey. Boring.

She walked to the door and with an almighty roar, she hurled the rock onto the shop floor, right where she'd cried her tears. It shattered, pieces flying off in different directions.

Suddenly needing the safety and love of her family, Summer decided to head back home.

As she turned to leave, a strange creaking and groaning sounded behind her. It was followed by dripping and crumbling sounds, and once again Summer's heart raced.

Was it Amber? Was Amber here?

Inhaling deeply, Summer swivelled her head to look back inside.

There was no Amber, and the shop remained empty. Except for one thing that definitely hadn't been there before.

Walking over to where she'd thrown the rock, she couldn't believe what she saw.

There, leading down into the darkness beneath the floor, was a staircase.

Real gemstones

Diamond

♦ The hardest natural material in the world! Only a diamond can scratch another diamond.

♦ In fact, the word 'diamond' comes from the Greek word for 'unbreakable'.

Ruby

♦ The second hardest gemstone after diamonds.

♦ The word 'ruby' comes from the Latin *ruber* which means 'red'.

Pearl

♦ The only gemstone that comes from an animal! Pearls are made inside the shells of mussels and oysters.

♦ Some pearls can take seven years to form inside an oyster.

Amethyst

• Some amethysts are as big as cars!

• When an amethyst gets hot, it can lose its colour.

Amber

• The only gemstone that comes from trees!

• Amber is tree sap that has become hardened over time.

Alexandrite

• This stone changes colour depending on the light.

• It's sometimes described as 'emerald by day and ruby by night'.

Chapter 4

Summer blinked. She blinked again. Then, she rubbed her eyes.

She looked over her shoulder, at the door, at the dusty shop, and then back down at the staircase.

"What is happening?" she said aloud, her voice echoing in the empty space.

She chewed her lip hard until it hurt, but feeling pain at least meant she wasn't dreaming. This was real.

Did the staircase lead to a basement? A cellar?

Summer's eyes followed the steps until they were swallowed up by darkness. A strange smell wafted out of the hole: the scent of flowers and mud and the freshness of the air after rainfall, of smoke and rubbish. She remembered that confusing smell.

A thought flickered through her mind. She didn't like it, but she couldn't make it go away either.

Maybe Amber was down there with Summer's bike and her money.

Summer gulped.

Could that be possible? That the strange woman with the amber eyes and bewitching presence lived underground, beneath the shop?

It was highly unlikely.

Yet, still Summer wondered.

Sucking in a deep breath followed by a long, slow exhale, she made up her mind. One step after another, Summer descended the staircase. The shop floor gradually disappeared above her as the darkness beneath welcomed her, along with hot, humid air.

The staircase wasn't wide: she could easily touch the walls on either side. She ran her hands down them, helping to keep her balance as the light dwindled, making each new step harder to see. Soon the walls changed from rough dry bricks to a smooth and damp surface, with a sleekness that Summer guessed was wet mud.

"How far does this staircase go?" she asked out loud, more to hear her own voice than anything else. The sound bounced off the walls and back at her, bringing her no comfort at all.

Down, down, down she climbed, wishing she'd counted the stairs. She must have been walking for at least ten minutes.

"I should turn back," she whispered to herself. "This feels wrong."

But then, as she went to take her next step, her boot met level ground. She had reached the bottom. With her hands pressed firmly against the muddy walls, she glanced back up to the top of the staircase. Any light coming from the shop above was now a distant dot.

"I should go back," she said again. "But I've come this far –"

Chewing her lip, she made her choice and cautiously stepped into a gloomy tunnel, which curved this way and that.

After a minute or two, a large, twinkling cavern opened up in front of her. She paused at the entrance to the cavern, her jaw dropping open in amazement. It was like being inside the most enormous amethyst.

As her eyes adjusted, Summer made out other entrances all around the walls of the cavern, like the one she stood in. Light trickled in from some of them.

She looked up, spotting ledges all around the vast space and even more tunnel entrances leading onto each one. Summer also noticed grooves set in the walls, creating ladders that led up from the ground and onto each ledge.

There was something else, too. Glancing upwards, she noticed that objects were piled on the ledge closest to her.

Summer squinted. "What is up there?" she murmured.

She decided to investigate.

She crept into the cavern, pressing her back to the wall so she could keep an eye out for … for ….

She paused and chewed her lip. What should she keep an eye out for? Amber? Danger? What kind of danger? She had no idea what might be living in a place like this.

Before Summer took a further step, she removed one of her yellow gloves.

She left it on the ground beside the tunnel entrance, so she would know which tunnel led back to the staircase and the shop. She then crept towards the ladder that led up to the ledge and climbed to the top.

"Oh my goodness!" Summer exclaimed, crouching next to the pile of objects. "What is all this stuff?" She spotted cups and glasses, boxes and books, a battered old clock and a model aeroplane, a ragged teddy bear in a waistcoat, a watch and a large silver spoon. Coins, gems, ornaments and jewellery were scattered everywhere. There was also a delicate gold item that captured Summer's attention.

It was a necklace with a cat-shaped pendant attached. Why was it familiar?

A distant pattering in the cavern made her freeze. Eyes wide, she surveyed the vast space. Was it a mouse, or a rat maybe? When there were no further sounds or signs of movement anywhere, Summer exhaled and returned to considering this unusual necklace.

Then, the realisation hit her.

This was Mrs Barry's necklace. Sebastian had mentioned it yesterday, how it had been stolen.

More pattering echoed through the cavern. This time a little louder.

That was one big rat. At least Summer hoped it was a rat. Maybe it was time for her to leave.

Summer gathered the necklace in her hand and brushed off the dust. This was how she'd get back in Mrs Barry's good books. But just then …

"Wonderful things for me, wonderful things for me," sang a familiar voice.

Summer paused midway down the ladder. A bead of sweat trickled down the side of her head.

Amber *was* here.

"Wonderful things for me, wonderful things for me."

The more Summer listened to the words, the more she focused on where the pattering and the voice were coming from. Her breath caught in her throat. It sounded as if Amber was moving fast through one of the nearby tunnels – very, very fast.

Was Amber running? How could a person make their feet move that quickly?

"Wonderful things for me, wonderful –"

The voice cut off and an eerie feeling prickled up Summer's back and neck. Amber was close. Amber was watching her.

"Who is stealing my wonderful things?"

Summer stopped breathing, staying as quiet and still as possible.

"I can smell you, little girl."

Summer gulped and glanced over her shoulder. First at the tunnel marked by her yellow glove, and second at a shadow looming out of another tunnel.

"I can hear you, little girl."

Suddenly her bike and money didn't seem important.

Escaping was the only thing on her mind.

She counted down in her head.

Three …

Two …

Summer took one last look at the pile of objects on the platform, frowning as she spotted more and more things that seemed familiar.

The pattering drew closer. She didn't have any more time.

One …

Clutching the necklace, Summer ran.

Bonus: Wonderful things for me

Chapter 5

"I can see you, little girl," called Amber in a voice that no longer sounded at all human. *How could that be possible?* Summer asked herself. The pattering got louder and faster, now resembling ten sets of horses' hooves thundering in Summer's direction.

Summer did not look back. She sprinted through the entrance marked by her yellow glove and through the curving, winding tunnel until she finally reached the staircase.

"Wonderful things for me. Wonderful things for me," chanted Amber. She was gaining on Summer. Wiping sweat from her forehead, Summer dug deep and threw herself up the stairs two at a time.

Her thighs burned, her breath was ragged, but there was no way she would stop until she was back in the shop and out the door. She needed fresh air and familiar surroundings.

"Wonderful things for me," sang Amber, now right behind Summer.

The light from above poured onto the staircase. She was nearly there. Nearly back to safety.

With a final push and a bellow, she leapt up the final stairs and burst into the shop. Something cold brushed against her ankle. Summer screamed and kicked out, then stumbled through the shop door into daylight.

Outside, rain spat on her as she caught her breath. She faced the shop and, through the open door, watched a shadow inside slithering away. Amber's voice faded with it.

"Wonderful things for me."

Summer took several steps back, her eyes fixed on the doorway, but no one and nothing came out. She'd done it. She'd escaped.

The relief was wonderful. Summer almost felt like crying.

So many strange things had happened that made absolutely no sense. Summer needed to think and process it all. But first, she would return Mrs Barry's necklace.

That afternoon, Summer lay on her bed, twirling her one remaining yellow glove round and round in her hands. At the same time, the events of earlier twirled around in her mind.

How had the staircase got there?

What was Amber?

Did Amber live in the cavern?

Where did the other tunnels lead?

Why was Mrs Barry's necklace down there?

One more, final question arrived in her brain with a pop.

Could that have been Mr Johnston's missing teddy bear? It was wearing a tartan waistcoat after all.

Summer sat up slowly, several threads merging in her mind.

If Mrs Barry's necklace was down the staircase, along with Mr Johnston's teddy bear, could that mean *all* the other items stolen from the estate were there too?

Including Grandma's candlestick?

Amber had to be the thief. It was the only explanation.

Thinking hard, Summer stared down at her thick stripey socks and wiggled her toes. Then she brushed back her wild hair and looked at her reflection in her bedroom mirror.

"Maybe I should tell Dad. Or the police," she pondered. But, really, would they believe her? Would they act quickly enough?

"Or *I* could go back down there … back down the staircase." Summer chewed her lip. "Can I do it? Am I brave enough?"

There was only one answer to both these questions.

"Yes, I can. Yes, I am." She stood and clenched her fists. "I cannot let Amber get away with stealing and lying."

Summer threw on her warmest jumper, her scarf, and her one glove. She emptied out her school backpack and grabbed her reading torch from her bedside table.

Downstairs, Dad and Alfie snoozed on the sofa together. Rather than bother them, she left a detailed note telling Dad exactly where she had gone and that she'd call on her mobile if there were any problems, and then she quietly and carefully left the house.

With each step that brought her closer to the shop, determination and fright clashed inside Summer's body. One minute she wanted to run home, the next she wanted to get this over and done with.

She remembered the superfast pattering sound in the cavern, the eerie singing in a voice that wasn't at all human. What *was* Amber?

No, she told herself and shook away that thought.

Arriving at the shop for the second time that day, Summer felt a little wiser and more prepared than last time. After checking for Amber and other pattering creatures loitering in the shop or on the staircase, Summer made her way down towards the amethyst cavern. She pressed one hand firmly against the wall. The other gripped her tiny reading torch.

When she reached the bottom, she tiptoed as quickly and as quietly as she could through the tunnel until she emerged into the cavern at the other end. The yellow glove that she'd left there earlier was gone, so this time she placed her other glove on the ground.

Off she went, creeping around the edges of the cavern as she had before, eyes wide and ears alert. She was ready to run the moment she heard any pattering or singing. There was no way she wanted to find out what might happen if Amber caught her.

So far so good, Summer thought. She climbed the ladder and heaved herself onto the ledge. Everything looked just as she'd left it, including Mr Johnston's teddy bear. Summer picked it up.

"I'm taking you back home," Summer whispered to the teddy.

Opening her backpack, she placed the teddy inside and started to close the zip. She paused. There was plenty of space in her backpack, and no sign of Amber. So, Summer loaded up her backpack with items, including the silver spoon, the old clock and the watch, before scooping up handfuls of coins and gems.

There was room for one more thing. She studied the mound of remaining objects.

She gasped. Right there, buried in the middle, was Grandma's brass candlestick! Excited, she grabbed it too quickly. A glass fell and shattered on the ground.

"Oh no," Summer hissed. She held her breath, waiting, listening.

"Wonderful things for me. Wonderful things for me," chanted Amber, accompanied by that familiar pattering of feet.

Without wasting a further second, Summer rammed the candlestick inside her bag and rushed down the ladder.

"I smell you, little girl," Amber called.

Patter patter.

"I hear you, little girl."

Patter patter.

Summer leapt from the ladder and stumbled. Righting herself, she raced towards her glove and the tunnel that led to freedom, but something shiny glinted in the corner of her eye.

She turned her head. "My bike!" she cried, but the pattering was approaching fast.

"I'll get you this time, little girl," Amber cried. A shadow emerged from a tunnel across the cavern.

Summer didn't have time to pause for a moment. Her bike would have to stay.

And she ran.

Animal hoarders

These animals are known for collecting and hiding items.

Macaque monkeys

steal items from people like sunglasses, phones and food.

Decorator crabs

use objects they find as shelter such as sponges and yoghurt pots.

Octopuses

take shells from other animals to make shelters and also for fun.

Burrowing owls decorate their underground dens with bottle caps and tin foil.

Satin bowerbirds build a bower (a structure like a nest that males build from twigs and leaves) and decorate it with lots of blue items to match their feathers.

Magpies collect shiny, glittery things such as jewellery and trinkets.

Chapter 6

Launching herself from the staircase and into the shop, Summer splatted on her hands and knees. She twisted away, managing to escape Amber's cold hands snatching at her.

If they even *were* hands.

They didn't look like hands, or even anything fleshy or human.

Summer bundled through the shop door so fast she caught only a glimpse of whatever was behind her. Something dark, alive, like creeping, spindly shadows snaking back down the hole in the shop floor.

Summer savoured the cold air hitting her hot face as she sprinted towards home. Her full backpack bashed and clanked against her back. Once she was a safe distance away, she slowed to catch her breath and calm her drumming heart.

She smiled. "I did it," she said as she peered inside the backpack. "Now to return these stolen items."

Not knowing which item belonged to whom, Summer decided to take everything to the nearby church. Doing her best not to be seen, she emptied the contents into the lost property cupboard in the entrance hall. Then, she studied the candlestick in her hand.

Dad and Alfie would have woken from their nap by now and would probably be wondering where she was. Alfie and Summer loved an early evening walk on Saturdays, when it was quieter and the light was fading. She didn't want to miss that.

But still Summer hesitated. Two new thoughts circled her mind, getting louder and louder.

She wanted her bike back.

What if Amber continued to steal from the estate's residents?

Summer sighed. She couldn't let that happen. It wasn't fair. Stealing was wrong.

She left the candlestick with the other items in the lost property cupboard and filled her lungs with cold air. She didn't know how or why, but something told her she was the only person who could put a stop to this, once and for all.

Spinning on her heel, she changed direction and headed right back to the shop.

As Summer descended the staircase and wound through the muddy tunnel for the third time, it felt spookier than ever. Her senses worked hard to locate sounds, but nothing except a heavy stillness surrounded her.

It took every ounce of her effort to push on and reach the cavern. Again, the unnerving silence draped over her, with no pattering or singing. Summer peered around the glittering purple space.

Once again, her glove was gone, but she could see her bike, leant up against the wall. Summer worked out it was only twenty steps away, but how would she get the bike through the tunnel and up the staircase? It was barely wide enough for her, and she was low on energy.

Then there was the dilemma of stopping Amber. Summer was a twelve-year-old girl with no magical powers or superstrength. Amber was ….

Summer still didn't know.

Standing around not making decisions wasn't helping anyone. Summer removed her scarf to mark the tunnel this time, and crept towards her bike. When nothing leapt out at her, she relaxed. She placed her hands on the handlebars, and a rush of warmth spread through her body.

"Hi, bike," she whispered, stroking the seat.

Patter. Patter. Patter.

A prickle of shivers spread down Summer's back. Peering left and right, she pushed her bike towards the tunnel but then froze.

"I smell you, little girl," sang Amber's voice coming from the tunnel to the staircase. "Wonderful things for me, but not for you."

Summer's heart raced. She needed to lure Amber away.

"I hear you, little girl. Wonderful things for me."

The pattering and echoing words were getting louder. Summer mounted her bike. Amber could move fast, so if Summer wanted any chance of escape, she needed to be even faster.

"I see you, little girl."

Summer squeezed the handlebars and gritted her teeth. She counted down in her head.

Three, two, one …

Then she took off. As quickly as her tired legs could manage, she sped through the cavern.

Amber appeared. Not the human Summer had met in the shop, but a creature that looked half-ant, half-dragon. With eyes that flashed amber.

Summer pedalled faster. Amber chased after her, laughing with delight. "Wonderful things for me," she sang over and over.

Summer's legs were getting tired. She couldn't keep going around in circles, so she made a break for her tunnel, ducking through the entrance a short distance in front of Amber. She scraped against the walls with Amber in pursuit. The speed of her two wheels had helped her get ahead.

A dot of light filtered in from above. "The staircase," Summer gasped.

"Wonderful things for me," sang Amber.

Summer was on the home straight. She flung herself off her bike, lifted it with her last scrap of strength, and charged up the stairs. Her thighs and arms shrieked with pain. Her lungs howled with exhaustion. But she didn't stop.

Finally, the shop appeared – the best sight ever.

Amber clawed at Summer's ankles, singing, "Wonderful things for me."

Summer shoved her bike onto the shop floor. Amber's freezing touch wrapped around her leg and tried to drag her back down.

"Get off me!" Summer yelped, kicking out. "You thief!"

"Wonderful things for me," Amber gargled back.

Another sound reached Summer's ears. Voices, from outside the shop.

"Help! Help!" she screeched as loud as she could. "Help!"

"Summer? Is that you?"

"DAD!"

"Sunner!"

"ALFIE! In here!"

Footsteps drew closer and Amber's coldness slid away from Summer's leg.

Summer threw herself onto the shop floor. She scrabbled backwards and pushed herself to her feet.

Glancing back, Summer couldn't believe what she was seeing. The hole in the shop floor was shrinking, the staircase disappearing. She watched two sparkling amber eyes fade from sight until all that remained was the concrete floor.

As if the staircase had never existed.

Alfie burst through the shop door, followed by Dad.

"What are you doing here?" Dad asked, grimacing at Summer's mud-covered coat. He righted her discarded bike. "Are you OK?"

Summer caught her breath and nodded.

"Sure?"

Summer nodded again.

"Rock." Alfie thrust out his hand and unfurled his fingers.

Summer blinked. There in his palm sat an opal.

"But, how?" she asked.

Dad chuckled. "Eagle-eyed Alfie spotted it lying on the side of the path by the church."

Summer looked at the opal then at Alfie's and Dad's smiles, and then finally she focused on the satisfied feeling inside her. She'd done it!

"Lucky, huh?" Dad said. "Come on, let's walk home together."

As the three of them left the shop, Dad pulled the shop door closed behind them and Summer took one final look back.

For some reason that Summer couldn't fully explain, she felt certain they'd seen the last of Amber, forever.

A retelling

Summer and the Staircase is a retelling of the fairy tale *Jack and the Beanstalk.*

Here are some similarities between the two stories:

1 Being tricked

Jack hopes to get money for his cow, but he's tricked into selling it for magic beans.

Summer is tricked into buying a fake rock for her money and her bike.

2 Throwing away

Jack's mother throws the beans out of the window and a beanstalk grows up into the sky.

Summer throws the Catacombite on the floor of the shop and a staircase appears, heading underground.

3 Venturing

Jack climbs the beanstalk and finds a giant.

Summer descends the staircase to find a creature.

4 Stealing

Jack steals a bag of coins from the giant.

Summer takes back the gold cat necklace that Amber has stolen.

5 More stealing!

Jack climbs the beanstalk twice more and steals a hen that lays golden eggs followed by a magical harp.

Summer descends the stairs twice more and takes back a teddy bear, a silver spoon, a clock, a watch and a candlestick, followed by her bike.

6 Being chased

The giant chases Jack down the beanstalk.

Amber chases Summer up the staircase.

About the author

What made you want to be a writer?

I have always written stories and poems, since I was as young as four, but as I grew up I never thought it was possible for someone like me to be able to write for my job. But I was wrong! I now write to help people make sense of the world.

Kate Foster

What's the best and most challenging thing about writing?

The best thing is that most days I get to lie in bed, in my PJs, surrounded by my dogs, and make things up! The most challenging thing is having so many ideas for new stories but not knowing where to start!

How do you decide what a story will be about?

A lot of my stories are based on experiences that I've had in my life, sometimes small moments that have made me feel something very deeply. So that's usually where the idea starts. I am also inspired by scenes in movies and TV shows I watch, or characters I read about in other books. In my day-to-day life I love to ask, *I wonder what would happen if* ... It's so much fun! I now write to help people, especially autistic people like me who don't always feel seen or understood, make sense of the world. Autistic people deserve to star in exciting stories and show how brave and brilliant they are, too.

What was your favourite book when you were young?
I had so many favourite books, but I truly loved *The Worst Witch* series by Jill Murphy. I saw a lot of myself in Mildred Hubble!

Do any of the characters in this book relate to any real people you know?
A little bit, yes. Summer is definitely like me! As I put the skeleton of this story together and thought about the middle section and especially the end, I really wanted to challenge myself, and therefore Summer. I forced us both to make important decisions that would lean into our fears but also into our strengths and skills. People see certain characteristics as a weakness, but those same ones can end up being a strength.

Why did you want to write this story?
I love fairy tales, they are usually such dark stories that teach us important lessons, and Jack and the Beanstalk is one of my favourites. I love characters who persevere through the hardest times and who are driven to put things right no matter how afraid they are. We can all be courageous, especially when it comes to caring for those we love.

What do you hope readers will get from the book?
Mostly, I hope readers will have fun and maybe feel a little scared too! I also hope readers will learn that anyone can be brave and anyone can be a hero.

About the illustrator

Do you illustrate digitally, or with pens and paints?
I illustrate digitally. It's very convenient and fun! You can take your tablet anywhere and just sit down and draw!

Fran Cesarano

How did you decide what Summer Spriggins should look like?
I pictured her looks and style right away while reading the book just before illustrating. The author's words really brought her to life! Then as I worked on the character, I added other small touches to suit her personality.

What was the most challenging thing about illustrating this book?
Working out how to illustrate all the locations. The locations move from Summer's home, to her town and then to the shop. After that, things really get challenging as we venture underground!

What did you like best about illustrating this book?
I loved exploring the character designs! It was fun trying to imagine what different people and creatures might look like. The creepy hands reaching out were really fun to illustrate.

Do you base human characters on people you know?
I do, I base them on my closest friends and my loved ones. That way, it is easier to imagine the characters in different poses and with different expressions.

Which was your favourite scene to draw in the book?
I LOVED drawing Summer exploring the Amethyst cave and gathering all the missing objects. Caves are so mysterious and it was exciting to draw the inside of the cave with the maze of tunnels, entrances and exits.

Which was your favourite character to draw in the book?
Summer! She's so brave, and overcomes her fears – that makes people really interesting to draw.

Do you prefer to draw real places, or to use your imagination?
I prefer to use a combination of both. I use reference pictures to get inspiration, then when drawing I use my imagination.

Do you collect anything, like Summer and her family?
I am autistic and have ADHD, like Summer, and I collect trading cards! I have a huge collection. My partner and I love adding to the collection.

Book chat

What did you think this book might be about? Were you right?

Did you think the new shop was suspicious?

Do you have a favourite part in the book?

Did you find any parts of the story scary? Which bits?

If you had to think up a new title for this book, what would you choose?

If you could speak to any of the characters in the book, who would you choose and what would you ask?

What's your favourite illustration in the book? Why do you like it?

Which character do you relate to the most and why?

Book challenge:

Draw a maze-like map of the cave and ensure Summer has an escape route.

Published by Collins
An imprint of HarperCollins*Publishers*

The News Building
1 London Bridge Street
London
SE1 9GF
UK

Macken House
39/40 Mayor Street Upper
Dublin 1
D01 C9W8
Ireland

Text © Kate Foster 2025
Design and illustrations © HarperCollins*Publishers* Limited 2025

10 9 8 7 6 5 4 3 2 1

ISBN 978-0-00-876789-1

All rights reserved. No part of this publication may be reproduced, stored in a retrieval system, or transmitted in any form by any means, electronic, mechanical, photocopying, recording or otherwise, without the prior written permission of the Publisher or a licence permitting restricted copying in the United Kingdom issued by the Copyright Licensing Agency Ltd, 5th Floor, Shackleton House, 4 Battle Bridge Lane, London SE1 2HX.

Without limiting the exclusive rights of any author, contributor or the publisher of this publication, any unauthorised use of this publication to train generative artificial intelligence (AI) technologies is expressly prohibited. HarperCollins also exercise their rights under Article 4(3) of the Digital Single Market Directive 2019/790 and expressly reserve this publication from the text and data mining exception.

British Library Cataloguing-in-Publication Data
A catalogue record for this publication is available from the British Library.

Download the teaching notes and word cards to accompany this book at:
http://littlewandle.org.uk/signupfluency/

Get the latest Collins Big Cat news at
collins.co.uk/collinsbigcat

Author: Kate Foster
Illustrator: Fran Cesarano (Astound US)
Publisher: Laura White
Product managers: Caroline Green and
 Holly Woolnough
Series editor: Charlotte Raby
Development editor: Catherine Baker
Commissioning editor: Caroline Green
Project manager: Emily Hooton
Copyeditor: Sally Byford
Proofreader: Catherine Dakin
Cover designer: Sarah Finan
Typesetter: 2Hoots Publishing Services Ltd
Production controller: Sophie Waeland

Printed in the UK.

 MIX
Paper | Supporting responsible forestry
FSC
www.fsc.org   FSC™ C007454

This book contains FSC™ certified paper and other controlled sources to ensure responsible forest management.

For more information visit: www.harpercollins.co.uk/green

Made with responsibly sourced paper and vegetable ink

Scan to see how we are reducing our environmental impact.

Acknowledgements
The publishers gratefully acknowledge the permission granted to reproduce the copyright material in this book. Every effort has been made to trace copyright holders and to obtain their permission for the use of copyright material. The publishers will gladly receive any information enabling them to rectify any error or omission at the first opportunity.

p56t Alexander Maslennikov/Shutterstock, p56c Byjeng/Shutterstock, p56b STUDIO492/Shutterstock, p57t Pongsak14/Shutterstock, p57c ntv/Shutterstock, p57b Halyna Kubei/Alamy, p88t Will Falcon/Shutterstock, p88c corn-flower/Shutterstock, p88b Diego Grandi/Shutterstock, p89t Voodison328/Shutterstock, p89c Ken Griffiths/Shutterstock, p89b David Chapman/Alamy.